Third State of the Union Address

JAMES KNOX POLK

1847

TABLE OF CONTENTS

FELLOW-CITIZENS OF THE SENATE AND OF
THE HOUSE OF REPRESENTATIVES

FELLOW-CITIZENS OF THE SENATE AND OF THE HOUSE OF REPRESENTATIVES

The annual meeting of Congress is always an interesting event. The representatives of the States and of the people come fresh from their constituents to take counsel together for the common good.

After an existence of near three-fourths of a century as a free and independent Republic, the problem no longer remains to be solved whether man is capable of self-government. The success of our admirable system is a conclusive refutation of the theories of those in other countries who maintain that a "favored few" are born to rule and that the mass of mankind must be governed by force. Subject to no arbitrary or hereditary authority, the people are the only sovereigns recognized by our Constitution.

Numerous emigrants, of every lineage and language, attracted by the civil and religious freedom we enjoy and by our happy condition, annually crowd to our shores, and transfer their heart, not less than their allegiance, to the country whose dominion belongs alone to the people. No country has been so much favored, or should acknowledge with deeper reverence the manifestations of the divine protection. An all wise Creator directed and guarded us in our infant struggle for freedom and has constantly watched over our surprising progress until we have become one of the great nations of the earth.

It is in a country thus favored, and under a Government in which the executive and legislative branches hold their authority for limited periods alike from the people, and where all are responsible to their respective constituencies, that it is again my duty to communicate with Congress upon the state of the Union and the present condition of public affairs.

During the past year the most gratifying proofs are presented that our country has been blessed with a widespread and universal prosperity. There has been no period since the Government was founded when all the industrial pursuits of our people have been more successful or when labor in all branches of business has received a fairer or better reward. From our abundance we have been enabled to perform the pleasing duty of furnishing food for the starving millions of less favored countries.

In the enjoyment of the bounties of Providence at home such as have rarely fallen to the lot of any people, it is cause of congratulation that our intercourse with all the powers of the earth except Mexico continues to be of an amicable character.

It has ever been our cherished policy to cultivate peace and good will with all nations, and this policy has been steadily pursued by me. No change has taken place in our relations with Mexico since the adjournment of the last Congress. The war in which the United States were forced to engage with the Government of that country still continues.

I deem it unnecessary, after the full exposition of them contained in my message of the 11th of May, 1846, and in my annual message at the commencement of the session of Congress in December last, to reiterate the serious causes of complaint which we had against Mexico before she commenced hostilities.

It is sufficient on the present occasion to say that the wanton violation of the rights of person and property of our citizens committed by Mexico, her repeated acts of bad faith through a long series of years, and her disregard of solemn treaties stipulating for indemnity to our injured citizens not only constituted ample cause of war on our part, but were of such an aggravated character as would have justified us before the whole world in resorting to this extreme remedy. With an anxious desire to avoid a rupture between the two countries, we forbore for years to assert our clear rights by force, and continued to seek redress for the wrongs we had suffered by amicable negotiation in the hope that Mexico might yield to pacific counsels and the demands of justice. In this hope we were disappointed. Our minister of peace sent to Mexico was insultingly rejected. The Mexican Government refused even to hear the terms of adjustment which he was authorized to propose, and finally, under wholly unjustifiable pretexts, involved the two countries in war by invading the territory of the State of Texas, striking the first blow, and shedding the blood of our citizens on our own soil.

Though the United States were the aggrieved nation, Mexico commenced the war, and we were compelled in self-defense to repel the invader and to vindicate the national honor and interests by prosecuting it with vigor until we could obtain a just and honorable peace. On learning that hostilities had been commenced by Mexico I promptly communicated that fact, accompanied with a succinct statement of our other causes of complaint against Mexico, to Congress, and that body, by the act of the 13th of May, 1846, declared that "by the act of the Republic of Mexico a state of war exists between that Government and the United States." This act declaring "the war to exist by the act of the Republic of Mexico," and making provision for its prosecution "to a speedy and successful termination," was passed with great unanimity by Congress, there being but two negative votes in the Senate and but fourteen in the House of Representatives.

The existence of the war having thus been declared by Congress, it became my duty under the Constitution and the laws to conduct and prosecute it. This duty has been performed, and though at every stage of its progress I have manifested a willingness to terminate it by a just peace, Mexico has refused to accede to any terms which could be accepted by the United States consistently with the national honor and interest.

The rapid and brilliant successes of our arms and the vast extent of the enemy's territory which had been overrun and conquered before the close of the last session of Congress were fully known to that body. Since that time the war has been prosecuted with increased energy, and, I am gratified to state, with a success which commands universal admiration.. History presents no parallel of so many glorious victories achieved by any nation within so short a period. Our Army, regulars and volunteers, have covered themselves with imperishable honors. Whenever and wherever our forces have encountered the enemy, though he was in vastly superior numbers and often intrenched in fortified positions of his own selection and of great strength, he has been defeated. Too much praise can not be bestowed upon our officers and men, regulars and volunteers, for their gallantry, discipline, indomitable courage, and perseverance, all seeking the post of danger and vying with each other in deeds of noble daring.

While every patriot's heart must exult and a just national pride animate every bosom in beholding the high proofs of courage, consummate military skill, steady discipline, and humanity to the vanquished enemy exhibited by our gallant Army, the nation is called to mourn over the loss of many brave officers and soldiers, who have fallen in defense of their country's honor and interests. The brave dead met their melancholy fate in a foreign land, nobly discharging their duty, and with their country's flag waving triumphantly in the face of the foe. Their patriotic deeds are justly appreciated, and will long be remembered by their grateful countrymen. The parental care of the Government they loved and served should be extended to their surviving families.

Shortly after the adjournment of the last session of Congress the gratifying intelligence was received of the signal victory of Buena Vista, and of the fall of the city of Vera Cruz, and with it the strong castle of San Juan de Ulloa, by which it was defended. Believing that after these and other successes so honorable to our arms and so disastrous to Mexico the period was propitious to afford her another opportunity, if she thought proper to embrace it, to enter into negotiations for peace, a commissioner was appointed to proceed to the headquarters of our Army with full powers to enter upon negotiations and to conclude a just and honorable treaty of peace. He was not directed to make any new overtures of peace, but was the bearer of a dispatch from the Secretary of State of the United States to the minister of foreign affairs of Mexico, in reply to one received from the latter of the 22d of February, 1847, in which the Mexican Government was informed of his appointment and of his presence at the headquarters of our Army, and that he was invested with full powers to conclude a definitive treaty of peace whenever the Mexican Government might signify a desire to do so. While I was unwilling to subject the United States to another indignant refusal, I was yet resolved that the evils of the war should not be protracted a day longer than might be rendered absolutely necessary by the Mexican Government.

Care was taken to give no instructions to the commissioner which could in any way interfere with our military operations or relax our energies in the prosecution of the war. He possessed no authority in any manner to control these operations. He was authorized to exhibit his instructions to the general in command of the Army, and in the event of a treaty being concluded and ratified on the part of Mexico he was directed to give him notice of that fact. On the happening of such contingency, and on receiving notice thereof, the general in command was instructed by the Secretary of War to suspend further active military operations until further orders. These instructions were given with a view to intermit hostilities until the treaty thus ratified by Mexico could be transmitted to Washington and receive the action of the Government of the United States. The commissioner was also directed on reaching the Army to deliver to the general in command the dispatch which he bore from the Secretary of State to the minister of foreign affairs of Mexico, and on receiving it the general was instructed by the Secretary of War to cause it to be transmitted to the commander of the Mexican forces, with a quest that it might be communicated to his Government. The commissioner did not reach the headquarters of the Army until after another brilliant victory had crowned our arms at Cerro Gordo. The dispatch which he bore from the Secretary of War to the general in command of the Army was received by that officer, then at Jalapa, on the 7th of May, 1847, together with the dispatch from the Secretary of State to the minister of foreign affairs of Mexico, having been transmitted to him from Vera Cruz. The commissioner arrived at the headquarters of the Army a few days afterwards. His presence with the Army and his diplomatic character were made known to the Mexican Government from Puebla on the 12th of June, 1847, by the transmission of the dispatch from the Secretary of State to the minister of foreign affairs of Mexico.

Many weeks elapsed after its receipt, and no overtures were made nor was any desire expressed by the Mexican Government to enter into negotiations for peace.

Our Army pursued its march upon the capital, and as it approached it was met by formidable resistance. Our forces first encountered the enemy, and achieved signal victories in the severely contested battles of Contreras and Churubusco. It was not until after these actions had resulted in decisive victories and the capital of the enemy was within our power that the Mexican Government manifested any disposition to enter into negotiations for peace, and even then, as events have proved, there is too much reason to believe they were insincere, and that in agreeing to go through the forms of negotiation the object was to gain time to strengthen the defenses of their capital and to prepare for fresh resistance.

The general in command of the Army deemed it expedient to suspend hostilities temporarily by entering into an armistice with a view to the opening of negotiations. Commissioners were appointed on the part of Mexico to meet the commissioner on the part of the United States. The result of the conferences which took place between these functionaries of the two Governments was a failure to conclude a treaty of peace. The commissioner of the United States took with him the project of a treaty already prepared, by the terms of which the indemnity required by the United States was a cession of territory.

It is well known that the only indemnity which it is in the power of Mexico to make in satisfaction of the just and long-deferred claims of our citizens against her and the only means by which she can reimburse the United States for the expenses of the war is a cession to the United States of a portion of her territory. Mexico has no money to pay, and no other means of making the required indemnity. If we refuse this, we can obtain nothing else. To reject indemnity by refusing to accept a cession of territory would be to abandon all our just demands, and to wage the war, bearing all its expenses, without a purpose or definite object.

A state of war abrogates treaties previously existing between the belligerents and a treaty of peace puts an end to all claims for indemnity for tortious acts committed under the authority of one government against the citizens or subjects of another unless they are provided for in its stipulations. A treaty of peace which would terminate the existing war without providing for indemnity would enable Mexico, the acknowledged debtor and herself the aggressor in the war, to relieve herself from her just liabilities. By such a treaty our citizens who hold just demands against her would have no remedy either against Mexico or their own Government. Our duty to these citizens must forever prevent such a peace, and no treaty which does not provide ample means of discharging these demands can receive my sanction.

A treaty of peace should settle all existing differences between the two countries. If an adequate cession of territory should be made by such a treaty, the United States should release Mexico from all her liabilities and assume their payment to our own citizens. If instead of this the United States were to consent to a treaty by which Mexico should again engage to pay the heavy amount of indebtedness which a just indemnity to our Government and our citizens would impose on her, it is notorious that she does not possess the means to meet such an undertaking. From such a treaty no result could be anticipated but the same irritating disappointments which have heretofore attended the violations of similar treaty stipulations on the part of Mexico. Such a treaty would be but a temporary cessation of hostilities, without the restoration of the friendship and good understanding which should characterize the future intercourse between the two countries.

That Congress contemplated the acquisition of territorial indemnity when that body made provision for the prosecution of the war is obvious. Congress could not have meant when, in May, 1846, they appropriated $10,000,000 and authorized the President to employ the militia and naval and military forces of the United States and to accept the services of 50,000 volunteers to enable him to prosecute the war, and when, at their last session, and after our Army had invaded Mexico, they made additional appropriations and authorized the raising of additional troops for the same purpose, that no indemnity was to be obtained from Mexico at the conclusion of the war; and yet it was certain that if no Mexican territory was acquired no indemnity could be obtained. It is further manifest that Congress contemplated territorial indemnity from the fact that at their last session an act was passed, upon the Executive recommendation, appropriating $3,000,000 with that express object. This appropriation was made "to enable the President to conclude a treaty of peace, limits, and boundaries with the Republic of Mexico, to be used by him in the event that said treaty, when signed by the authorized agents of the two Governments and duly ratified by Mexico, shall call for the expenditure of the same or any part thereof." The object of asking this appropriation was distinctly stated in the several messages on the subject which I communicated to Congress. Similar appropriations made in 1803 and 1806, which were referred to, were intended to be applied in part consideration for the cession of Louisiana and the Floridas. In like manner it was anticipated that in settling the terms of a treaty of "limits and boundaries" with Mexico a cession of territory estimated to be of greater value than the amount of our demands against her might be obtained, and that the prompt payment of this sum in part consideration for the territory ceded, on the conclusion of a treaty and its ratification on her part, might be an inducement with her to make such a cession of territory as would be satisfactory to the United States; and although the failure to conclude such a treaty has rendered it unnecessary to use any part of the $3,000,000 appropriated by that act, and the entire sum remains in the Treasury, it is still applicable to that object should the contingency occur making such application proper.

The doctrine of no territory is the doctrine of no indemnity, and if sanctioned would be a public acknowledgment that our country was wrong and that the war declared by Congress with extraordinary unanimity was unjust and should be abandoned-an admission unfounded in fact and degrading to the national character.

The terms of the treaty proposed by the United States were not only just to Mexico, but, considering the character and amount of our claims, the unjustifiable and unprovoked commencement of hostilities by her, the expenses of the war to which we have been subjected, and the success which had attended our arms, were deemed to be of a most liberal character.

The commissioner of the United States was authorized to agree to the establishment of the Rio Grande as the boundary from its entrance into the

Gulf to its intersection with the southern boundary of New Mexico, in north latitude about 32 degree, and to obtain a cession to the United States of the Provinces of New Mexico and the Californias and the privilege of the right of way across the Isthmus of Tehuantepec. The boundary of the Rio Grande and the cession to the United States of New Mexico and Upper California constituted an ultimatum which our commissioner was under no circumstances to yield.

That it might be manifest, not only to Mexico, but to all other nations, that the United States were not disposed to take advantage of a feeble power by insisting upon wrestling from her all the other Provinces, including many of her principal towns and cities, which we had conquered and held in our military occupation but were willing to conclude a treaty in a spirit of liberality, our commissioner was authorized to stipulate for the restoration to Mexico of all our other conquests.

As the territory to be acquired by the boundary proposed might be estimated to be of greater value than a fair equivalent for our just demands, our commissioner was authorized to stipulate for the payment of such additional pecuniary consideration as was deemed reasonable.

The terms of a treaty proposed by the Mexican commissioners were wholly inadmissible. They negotiated as if Mexico were the victorious, and not the vanquished, party. They must have known that their ultimatum could never be accepted. It required the United States to dismember Texas by surrendering to Mexico that part of the territory of that State lying between the Nueces and the Rio Grande, included within her limits by her laws when she was an independent republic, and when she was annexed to the United States and admitted by Congress as one of the States of our Union. It contained no provision for the payment by Mexico of the just claims of our citizens. It required indemnity to Mexican citizens for injuries they may have sustained by our troops in the prosecution of the war. It demanded the right for Mexico to levy and collect the Mexican tariff of duties on goods imported into her ports while in our military occupation during the war, and the owners of which had paid to officers of the United States the military contributions which had been levied upon them; and it offered to cede to the United States, for a pecuniary consideration, that part of Upper California lying north of latitude 37°. Such were the unreasonable terms proposed by the Mexican commissioners.

The cession to the United States by Mexico of the Provinces of New Mexico and the Californias, as proposed by the commissioner of the United States, it was believed would be more in accordance with the convenience and interests of both nations than any other cession of territory which it was probable Mexico could be induced to make.

It is manifest to all who have observed the actual condition of the Mexican Government for some years past and at present that if these Provinces should be retained by her she could not long continue to hold and govern them. Mexico is too feeble a power to govern these Provinces, lying as they do at a distance of more than 1,000 miles from her capital, and if attempted to be retained by her they would constitute but for a short time even nominally a part of her dominions. This would be especially the case with Upper California.

The sagacity of powerful European nations has long since directed their attention to the commercial importance of that Province, and there can be little doubt that the moment the United States shall relinquish their present occupation of it and their claim to it as indemnity an effort would be made by some foreign power to possess it, either by conquest or by purchase. If no foreign government should acquire it in either of these modes, an independent revolutionary government would probably be established by the inhabitants and such foreigners as may remain in or remove to the country as soon as it shall be known that the United States have abandoned it. Such a government would be too feeble long to maintain its separate independent existence, and would finally become annexed to or be a dependent colony of some more powerful state. Should any foreign government attempt to possess it as a colony, or otherwise to incorporate it with itself, the principle avowed by President Monroe in 1824, and reaffirmed in my first annual message, that no foreign power shall with our consent be permitted to plant or establish any new colony or dominion on any part of the North American continent must be maintained. In maintaining this principle and in resisting its invasion by any foreign power we might be involved in other wars more expensive and more difficult than that in which we are now engaged. The Provinces of New Mexico and the Californias are contiguous to the territories of the United States, and if brought under the government of our laws their resources-mineral, agricultural, manufacturing, and commercial-would soon be developed.

Upper California is bounded on the north by our Oregon possessions, and if held by the United States would soon be settled by a hardy, enterprising, and intelligent portion of our population. The Bay of San Francisco and other harbors along the Californian coast would afford shelter for our Navy, for our numerous whale ships, and other merchant vessels employed in the Pacific Ocean, and would in a short period become the marts of an extensive and profitable commerce with China and other countries of the

East.

These advantages, in which the whole commercial world would participate, would at once be secured to the United States by the cession of this territory; while it is certain that as long as it remains a part of the Mexican dominions they can be enjoyed neither by Mexico herself nor by any other nation.

New Mexico is a frontier Province, and has never been of any considerable value to Mexico. From its locality it is naturally connected with our Western settlements. The territorial limits of the State of Texas, too, as defined by her laws before her admission into our Union, embrace all that portion of New Mexico lying east of the Rio Grande, while Mexico still claims to hold this territory as a part of her dominions. The adjustment of this question of boundary is important.

There is another consideration which induced the belief that the Mexican Government might even desire to place this Province under the protection of the Government of the United States. Numerous bands of fierce and warlike savages wander over it and upon its borders. Mexico has been and must continue to be too feeble to restrain them from committing depredations, robberies, and murders, not only upon the inhabitants of New Mexico itself, but upon those of the other northern States of Mexico. It would be a blessing to all these northern States to have their citizens protected against them by the power of the United States. At this moment many Mexicans, principally females and children, are in captivity among them. If New Mexico were held and governed by the United States, we could effectually prevent these tribes from committing such outrages, and compel them to release these captives and restore them to their families and friends.

In proposing to acquire New Mexico and the Californias, it was known that but an inconsiderable portion of the Mexican people would be transferred with them, the country embraced within these Provinces being chiefly an uninhabited region.

These were the leading considerations which induced me to authorize the terms of peace which were proposed to Mexico. They were rejected, and, negotiations being at an end, hostilities were renewed. An assault was made by our gallant Army upon the strongly fortified places near the gates of the City of Mexico and upon the city itself, and after several days of severe conflict the Mexican forces, vastly superior in number to our own, were driven from the city, and it was occupied by our troops.

Immediately after information was received of the unfavorable result of the negotiations, believing that his continued presence with the Army could be productive of no good, I determined to recall our commissioner. A dispatch to this effect was transmitted to him on the 6th of October last. The Mexican Government will be informed of his recall, and that in the existing state of things I shall not deem it proper to make any further overtures of peace, but shall be at all times ready to receive and consider any proposals which may be made by Mexico.

Since the liberal proposition of the United States was authorized to be made, in April last, large expenditures have been incurred and the precious blood of many of our patriotic fellow-citizens has been shed in the prosecution of the war. This consideration and the obstinate perseverance of Mexico in protracting the war must influence the terms of peace which it may be deemed proper hereafter to accept. Our arms having been everywhere victorious, having subjected to our military occupation a large portion of the enemy's country, including his capital, and negotiations for peace having failed, the important questions arise, in what manner the war ought to be prosecuted and what should be our future policy. I can not doubt that we should secure and render available the conquests which we have already made, and that with this view we should hold and occupy by our naval and military forces all the ports, towns, cities, and Provinces now in our occupation or which may hereafter fall into our possession; that we should press forward our military operations and levy such military contributions on the enemy as may, as far as practicable, defray the future expenses of the war.

Had the Government of Mexico acceded to the equitable and liberal terms proposed, that mode of adjustment would have been preferred, Mexico having declined to do this and failed to offer any other terms which could be accepted by the United States, the national honor, no less than the public interests, requires that the war should be prosecuted with increased energy and power until a just and satisfactory peace can be obtained. In the meantime, as Mexico refuses all indemnity, we should adopt measures to indemnify ourselves by appropriating permanently a portion of her territory. Early after the commencement of the war New Mexico and the Californias were taken possession of by our forces. Our military and naval commanders were ordered to conquer and hold them, subject to be disposed of by a treaty of peace.

These Provinces are now in our undisputed occupation, and have been so for many months, all resistance on the part of Mexico having ceased within their limits. I am satisfied that they should never be surrendered to Mexico. Should Congress concur with me in this opinion, and that they should be retained by the United States as indemnity, I can perceive no good reason why the civil jurisdiction and laws of the United States should not at once be extended over them. To wait for a treaty of peace such as we are willing to make, by which our relations toward them would not be changed, can not be good policy; whilst our own interest and that of the people inhabiting them require that a stable, responsible, and free government under our authority should as soon as possible be established over them. Should Congress, therefore, determine to hold these Provinces permanently, and that they shall hereafter be considered as constituent parts of our country, the early establishment of Territorial governments over them will be important for the more perfect protection of persons and property; and I recommend that such Territorial governments be established. It will promote peace and tranquillity among the inhabitants, by allaying all apprehension that they may still entertain of being again subjected to the jurisdiction of Mexico. I invite the early and favorable consideration of Congress to this important subject.

Besides New Mexico and the Californias, there are other Mexican Provinces which have been reduced to our possession by conquest. These other Mexican Provinces are now governed by our military and naval commanders under the general authority which is conferred upon a conqueror by the laws of war. They should continue to be held, as a means of coercing Mexico to accede to just terms of peace. Civil as well as military officers are required to conduct such a government. Adequate compensation, to be drawn from contributions levied on the enemy, should be fixed by law for such officers as may be thus employed. What further provision may become necessary and what final disposition it may be proper to make of them must depend on the future progress of the war and the course which Mexico may think proper hereafter to pursue.

With the views I entertain I can not favor the policy which has been suggested, either to withdraw our Army altogether or to retire to a designated line and simply hold and defend it. To withdraw our Army altogether from the conquests they have made by deeds of unparalleled bravery, and at the expense of so much blood and treasure, in a just war on our part, and one which, by the act of the enemy, we could not honorably have avoided, would be to degrade the nation in its own estimation and in that of the world. To retire to a line and simply hold and defend it would not terminate the war. On the contrary, it would encourage Mexico to persevere and tend to protract it indefinitely. It is not to be expected that Mexico, after refusing to establish such a line as a permanent boundary when our victorious Army are in possession of her capital and in the heart of her country, would permit us to hold it without resistance. That she would continue the war, and in the most harassing and annoying forms, there can be no doubt. A border warfare of the most savage character, extending over a long line, would be unceasingly waged. It would require a large army to be kept constantly in the field, stationed at posts and garrisons along such a line, to protect and defend it. The enemy, relieved from the pressure of our arms on his coasts and in the populous parts of the interior, would direct his attention to this line, and, selecting an isolated post for attack, would concentrate his forces upon it. This would be a condition of affairs which the Mexicans, pursuing their favorite system of guerrilla warfare, would probably prefer to any other. Were we to assume a defensive attitude on such a line, all the advantages of such a state of war would be on the side of the enemy. We could levy no contributions upon him, or in any other way make him feel the pressure of the war, but must remain inactive and await his approach, being in constant uncertainty at what point on the line or at what time he might make an assault. He may assemble and organize an overwhelming force in the interior on his own side of the line, and, concealing his purpose, make a sudden assault upon some one of our posts so distant from any other as to prevent the possibility of timely succor or reenforcements, and in this way our gallant Army would be exposed to the danger of being cut off in detail; or if by their unequaled bravery and prowess everywhere exhibited during this war they should repulse the enemy, their numbers stationed at any one post may be too small to pursue him. If the enemy be repulsed in one attack, he would have nothing to do but to retreat to his own side of the line, and, being in no fear of a pursuing army, may reenforce himself at leisure for another attack on the same or some other post. He may, too, cross the line between our posts, make rapid incursions into the country which we hold, murder the inhabitants, commit depredations on them, and then retreat to the interior before a sufficient force can be concentrated to pursue him. Such would probably be the harassing character of a mere defensive war on our part. If our forces when attacked, or threatened with attack, be permitted to cross the line, drive back the enemy, and conquer him, this would be again to invade the enemy's country after having lost all the advantages of the conquests we have already made by having voluntarily abandoned them. To hold such a line successfully and in security it is far from being certain that it would not require as large an army as would be necessary to hold all the conquests we have already made and to continue the prosecution of the war in the heart of the enemy's country. It is also far from being certain that the expenses of the war would be diminished by such a policy. I am persuaded that the best means of vindicating the national honor and interest and of bringing the war to an honorable close will be to prosecute it with increased energy and power in the vital parts of the enemy's country.

In my annual message to Congress of December last I declared that- The war has not been waged with a view to conquest, but, having been commenced by Mexico, it has been carried into the enemy's country and will be vigorously prosecuted there with a view to obtain an honorable peace, and thereby secure ample indemnity for the expenses of the war, as well as to our much-injured citizens, who hold large pecuniary demands against Mexico.

Such, in my judgment, continues to be our true policy; indeed, the only policy which will probably secure a permanent peace.

It has never been contemplated by me, as an object of the war, to make a permanent conquest of the Republic of Mexico or to annihilate her separate existence as an independent nation. On the contrary, it has ever been my desire that she should maintain her nationality, and under a good government adapted to her condition be a free, independent, and prosperous Republic. The United States were the first among the nations to recognize her independence, and have always desired to be on terms of amity and good neighborhood with her. This she would not suffer. By her own conduct we have been compelled to engage in the present war. In its prosecution we seek not her overthrow as a nation, but in vindicating our national honor we seek to obtain redress for the wrongs she has done us and indemnity for our just demands against her. We demand an honorable peace, and that peace must bring with it indemnity for the past and security for the future. Hitherto Mexico has refused all accommodation by which such a peace could be obtained.

Whilst our armies have advanced from victory to victory from the commencement of the war, it has always been with the olive branch of peace in their hands, and it has been in the power of Mexico at every step to arrest hostilities by accepting it.

One great obstacle to the attainment of peace has undoubtedly arisen from the fact that Mexico has been so long held in subjection by one faction or military usurper after another, and such has been the condition of insecurity in which their successive governments have been placed that each has been deterred from making peace lest for this very cause a rival faction might expel it from power. Such was the fate of President Herrera's administration in 1845 for being disposed even to listen to the overtures of the United States to prevent the war, as is fully confirmed by an official correspondence which took place in the month of August last between him and his Government, a copy of which is herewith communicated. "For this cause alone the revolution which displaced him from power was set on foot" by General Paredes. Such may be the condition of insecurity of the present Government.

There can be no doubt that the peaceable and well-disposed inhabitants of Mexico are convinced that it is the true interest of their country to conclude an honorable peace with the United States, but the apprehension of becoming the victims of some military faction or usurper may have prevented them from manifesting their feelings by any public act. The removal of any such apprehension would probably cause them to speak their sentiments freely and to adopt the measures necessary for the restoration of peace. With a people distracted and divided by contending factions and a Government subject to constant changes by successive revolutions, the continued successes of our arms may fail to secure a satisfactory peace. In such event it may become proper for our commanding generals in the field to give encouragement and assurances of protection to the friends of peace in Mexico in the establishment and maintenance of a free republican government of their own choice, able and willing to conclude a peace which would be just to them and secure to us the indemnity we demand. This may become the only mode of obtaining such a peace. Should such be the result, the war which Mexico has forced upon us would thus be converted into an enduring blessing to herself. After finding her torn and distracted by factions, and ruled by military usurpers, we should then leave her with a republican government in the enjoyment of real independence and domestic peace and prosperity, performing all her relative duties in the great family of nations and promoting her own happiness by wise laws and their faithful execution.

If, after affording this encouragement and protection, and after all the persevering and sincere efforts we have made from the moment Mexico commenced the war, and prior to that time, to adjust our differences with her, we shall ultimately fail, then we shall have exhausted all honorable means in pursuit of peace, and must continue to occupy her country with our troops, taking the full measure of indemnity into our own hands, and must enforce the terms which our honor demands.

To act otherwise in the existing state of things in Mexico, and to withdraw our Army without a peace, would not only leave all the wrongs of which we complain unredressed, but would be the signal for new and fierce civil dissensions and new revolutions-all alike hostile to peaceful relations with the United States. Besides, there is danger, if our troops were withdrawn before a peace was conducted, that the Mexican people, wearied with successive revolutions and deprived of protection for their persons and property, might at length be inclined to yield to foreign influences and to cast themselves into the arms of some European monarch for protection from the anarchy and suffering which would ensue. This, for our own safety and in pursuance of our established policy, we should be compelled to resist. We could never consent that Mexico should be thus converted into a monarchy governed by a foreign prince.

Mexico is our near neighbor, and her boundaries are coterminous with our own through the whole extent across the North American continent, from ocean to ocean. Both politically and commercially we have the deepest interest in her regeneration and prosperity. Indeed, it is impossible that, with any just regard to our own safety, we can ever become indifferent to her fate.

It may be that the Mexican Government and people have misconstrued or misunderstood our forbearance and our objects in desiring to conclude an amicable adjustment of the existing differences between the two countries. They may have supposed that we would submit to terms degrading to the nation, or they may have drawn false inferences from the supposed division of opinion in the United States on the subject of the war, and may have calculated to gain much by protracting it, and, indeed, that we might ultimately abandon it altogether without insisting on any indemnity, territorial or otherwise. Whatever may be the false impressions under which they have acted, the adoption and prosecution of the energetic policy proposed must soon undeceive them.

In the future prosecution of the war the enemy must be made to feel its pressure more than they have heretofore done. At its commencement it was deemed proper to conduct it in a spirit of forbearance and liberality. With this end in view, early measures were adopted to conciliate, as far as a state of war would permit, the mass of the Mexican population; to convince them that the war was waged, not against the peaceful inhabitants of Mexico, but against their faithless Government, which had commenced hostilities; to remove from their minds the false impressions which their designing and interested rulers had artfully attempted to make, that the war on our part was one of conquest, that it was a war against their religion and their churches, which were to be desecrated and overthrown, and that their rights of person and private property would be violated. To remove these false impressions, our commanders in the field were directed scrupulously to respect their religion, their churches, and their church property, which were in no manner to be violated; they were directed also to respect the rights of persons and property of all who should not take up arms against us.

Assurances to this effect were given to the Mexican people by Major General Taylor in a proclamation issued in pursuance of instructions from the Secretary of War in the month of June, 1846, and again by Major-General Scott, who acted upon his own convictions of the propriety of issuing it, in a proclamation of the 11th of May, 1847. In this spirit of liberality and conciliation, and with a view to prevent the body of the Mexican population from taking up arms against us, was the war conducted on our part. Provisions and other supplies furnished to our Army by Mexican citizens were paid for at fair and liberal prices, agreed upon by the parties. After the lapse of a few months it became apparent that these assurances and this mild treatment had failed to produce the desired effect upon the Mexican population. While the war had been conducted on our part according to the most humane and liberal principles observed by civilized nations, it was waged in a far different spirit on the part of Mexico. Not appreciating our forbearance, the Mexican people generally became hostile to the United States, and availed themselves of every opportunity to commit the most savage excesses upon our troops. Large numbers of the population took up arms, and, engaging in guerrilla warfare, robbed and murdered in the most cruel manner individual soldiers or small parties whom accident or other causes had separated from the main body of our Army; bands of guerrilleros and robbers infested the roads, harassed our trains, and whenever it was in their power cut off our supplies.

The Mexicans having thus shown themselves to be wholly incapable of appreciating our forbearance and liberality, it was deemed proper to change the manner of conducting the war, by making them feel its pressure according to the usages observed under similar circumstances by all other civilized nations.

Accordingly, as early as the 22d of September, 1846, instructions were given by the Secretary of War to Major-General Taylor to "draw supplies" for our Army "from the enemy without paying for them, and to require contributions for its support, if in that way he was satisfied he could get abundant supplies for his forces." In directing the execution of these instructions much was necessarily left to the discretion of the commanding officer, who was best acquainted with the circumstances by which he was surrounded, the wants of the Army, and the practicability of enforcing the measure. General Taylor, on the 26th of October, 1846, replied from Monterey that "it would have been impossible hitherto, and is so now, to sustain the Army to any extent by forced contributions of money or supplies." For the reasons assigned by him, he did not adopt the policy of his instructions, but declared his readiness to do so "should the Army in its future operations reach a portion of the country which may be made to supply the troops with advantage." He continued to pay for the articles of supply which were drawn from the enemy's country.

Similar instructions were issued to Major-General Scott on the 3d of April, 1847, who replied from Jalapa on the 20th of May, 1847, that if it be expected "that the Army is to support itself by forced contributions levied upon the country we may ruin and exasperate the inhabitants and starve ourselves." The same discretion was given to him that had been to General Taylor in this respect. General Scott, for the reasons assigned by him, also continued to pay for the articles of supply for the Army which were drawn from the enemy.

After the Army had reached the heart of the most wealthy portion of Mexico it was supposed that the obstacles which had before that time prevented it would not be such as to render impracticable the levy of forced contributions for its support, and on the 1st of September and again on the 6th of October, 1847, the order was repeated in dispatches addressed by the Secretary of War to General Scott, and his attention was again called to the importance of making the enemy bear the burdens of the war by requiring them to furnish the means of supporting our Army, and he was directed to adopt this policy unless by doing so there was danger of depriving the Army of the necessary supplies. Copies of these dispatches were forwarded to General Taylor for his government.

On the 31st of March last I caused an order to be issued to our military and naval commanders to levy and collect a military contribution upon all vessels and merchandise which might enter any of the ports of Mexico in our military occupation, and to apply such contributions toward defraying the expenses of the war. By virtue of the right of conquest and the laws of war, the conqueror, consulting his own safety or convenience, may either exclude foreign commerce altogether from all such ports or permit it upon such terms and conditions as he may prescribe. Before the principal ports of Mexico were blockaded by our Navy the revenue derived from import duties under the laws of Mexico was paid into the Mexican treasury. After these ports had fallen into our military possession the blockade was raised and commerce with them permitted upon prescribed terms and conditions. They were opened to the trade of all nations upon the payment of duties more moderate in their amount than those which had been previously levied by Mexico, and the revenue, which was formerly paid into the Mexican treasury, was directed to be collected by our military and naval officers and applied to the use of our Army and Navy. Care was taken that the officers, soldiers, and sailors of our Army and Navy should be exempted from the operations of the order, and, as the merchandise imported upon which the order operated must be consumed by Mexican citizens, the contributions exacted were in effect the seizure of the public revenues of Mexico and the application of them to our own use. In directing this measure the object was to compel the enemy to contribute as far as practicable toward the expenses of the war.

For the amount of contributions which have been levied in this form I refer you to the accompanying reports of the Secretary of War and of the Secretary of the Navy, by which it appears that a sum exceeding half a million of dollars has been collected. This amount would undoubtedly have been much larger but for the difficulty of keeping open communications between the coast and the interior, so as to enable the owners of the merchandise imported to transport and vend it to the inhabitants of the country. It is confidently expected that this difficulty will to a great extent be soon removed by our increased forces which have been sent to the field.

Measures have recently been adopted by which the internal as well as the external revenues of Mexico in all places in our military occupation will be seized and appropriated to the use of our Army and Navy.

The policy of levying upon the enemy contributions in every form consistently with the laws of nations, which it may be practicable for our military commanders to adopt, should, in my judgment, be rigidly enforced, and orders to this effect have accordingly been given. By such a policy, at the same time that our own Treasury will be relieved from a heavy drain, the Mexican people will be made to feel the burdens of the war, and, consulting their own interests, may be induced the more readily to require their rulers to accede to a just peace.

After the adjournment of the last session of Congress events transpired in the prosecution of the war which in my judgment required a greater number of troops in the field than had been anticipated. The strength of the Army was accordingly increased by "accepting" the services of all the volunteer forces authorized by the act of the 13th of May, 1846, without putting a construction on that act the correctness of which was seriously questioned. The volunteer forces now in the field, with those which had been "accepted" to "serve for twelve months" and were discharged at the end of their term of service, exhaust the 50,000 men authorized by that act. Had it been clear that a proper construction of the act warranted it, the services of an additional number would have been called for and accepted;

but doubts existing upon this point, the power was not exercised. It is deemed important that Congress should at an early period of their session confer the authority to raise an additional regular force to serve during the war with Mexico and to be discharged upon the conclusion and ratification of a treaty of peace. I invite the attention of Congress to the views presented by the Secretary of War in his report upon this subject.

I recommend also that authority be given by law to call for and accept the services of an additional number of volunteers, to be exercised at such time and to such extent as the emergencies of the service may require.

In prosecuting the war with Mexico, whilst the utmost care has been taken to avoid every just cause of complaint on the part of neutral nations, and none has been given, liberal privileges have been granted to their commerce in the ports of the enemy in our military occupation. The difficulty with the Brazilian Government, which at one time threatened to interrupt the friendly relations between the two countries, will, I trust, be speedily adjusted. I have received information that an envoy extraordinary and minister plenipotentiary to the United States will shortly be appointed by His Imperial Majesty, and it is hoped that he will come instructed and prepared to adjust all remaining differences between the two Governments in a manner acceptable and honorable to both. In the meantime, I have every reason to believe that nothing will occur to interrupt our amicable relations with Brazil.

It has been my constant effort to maintain and cultivate the most intimate relations of friendship with all the independent powers of South America, and this policy has been attended with the happiest results. It is true that the settlement and payment of many just claims of American citizens against these nations have been long delayed. The peculiar position in which they have been placed and the desire on the part of my predecessors as well as myself to grant them the utmost indulgence have hitherto prevented these claims from being urged in a manner demanded by strict justice. The time has arrived when they ought to be finally adjusted and liquidated, and efforts are now making for that purpose.

It is proper to inform you that the Government of Peru has in good faith paid the first two installments of the indemnity of $30,000 each, and the greater portion of the interest due thereon, in execution of the convention between that Government and the United States the ratifications of which were exchanged at Lima on the 31st of October, 1846. The Attorney-General of the United States early in August last completed the adjudication of the claims under this convention, and made his report thereon in pursuance of the act of the 8th of August, 1846. The sums to which the claimants are respectively entitled will be paid on demand at the Treasury.

I invite the early attention of Congress to the present condition of our citizens in China. Under our treaty with that power American citizens are withdrawn from the jurisdiction, whether civil or criminal, of the Chinese Government and placed under that of our public functionaries in that country. By these alone can our citizens be tried and punished for the commission of any crime; by these alone can questions be decided between them involving the rights of persons and property, and by these alone can contracts be enforced into which they may have entered with the citizens or subjects of foreign powers. The merchant vessels of the United States lying in the waters of the five ports of China open to foreign commerce are under the exclusive jurisdiction of officers of their own Government. Until Congress shall establish competent tribunals to try and punish crimes and to exercise jurisdiction in civil cases in China, American citizens there are subject to no law whatever. Crimes may be committed with impunity and debts may be contracted without any means to enforce their payment. Inconveniences have already resulted from the omission of Congress to legislate upon the subject, and still greater are apprehended. The British authorities in China have already complained that this Government has not provided for the punishment of crimes or the enforcement of contracts against American citizens in that country, whilst their Government has established tribunals by which an American citizen can recover debts due from British subjects. Accustomed, as the Chinese are, to summary justice, they could not be made to comprehend why criminals who are citizens of the United States should escape with impunity, in violation of treaty obligations, whilst the punishment of a Chinese who had committed any crime against an American citizen would be rigorously exacted. Indeed, the consequences might be fatal to American citizens in China should a flagrant crime be committed by any one of them upon a Chinese, and should trial and punishment not follow according to the requisitions of the treaty. This might disturb, if not destroy, our friendly relations with that Empire, and cause an interruption of our valuable commerce. Our treaties with the Sublime Porte, Tripoli, Tunis, Morocco, and Muscat also require the legislation of Congress to carry them into execution, though the necessity for immediate action may not be so urgent as in regard to China.

The Secretary of State has submitted an estimate to defray the expense of opening diplomatic relations with the Papal States. The interesting political events now in progress in these States, as well as a just regard to our commercial interests, have, in my opinion, rendered such a measure highly expedient.

Estimates have also been submitted for the outfits and salaries of charges' d'affaires to the Republics of Bolivia, Guatemala, and Ecuador. The manifest importance of cultivating the most friendly relations with all the independent States upon this continent has induced me to recommend appropriations necessary for the maintenance of these missions.

I recommend to Congress that an appropriation be made to be paid to the Spanish Government for the purpose of distribution among the claimants in the Amistad case. I entertain the conviction that this is due to Spain under the treaty of the 20th of October, 1795, and, moreover, that from the earnest manner in which the claim continues to be urged so long as it shall remain unsettled it will be a source of irritation and discord between the two countries, which may prove highly prejudicial to the interests of the United States. Good policy, no less than a faithful compliance with our treaty obligations, requires that the inconsiderable appropriation demanded should be made.

A detailed statement of the condition of the finances will be presented in the annual report of the Secretary of the Treasury. The imports for the last fiscal year, ending on the 30th of June, 1847, were of the value of $146,545,638, of which the amount exported was $8,011,158, leaving $138,534,480 in the country for domestic use. The value of the exports for the same period was $158,648,622, of which $150,637,464 consisted of domestic productions and $8,011,158 of foreign articles.

The receipts into the Treasury for the same period amounted to $26,346,790.37, of which there was derived from customs $23,747,864.66, from sales of public lands $2,498,335.20, and from incidental and miscellaneous sources $100,570.51. The last fiscal year, during which this amount was received, embraced five months under the operation of the tariff act of 1842 and seven months during which the tariff act of 1846 was in force. During the five months under the act of 1842 the amount received from customs was $7,842,306.90, and during the seven months under the act of 1846 the amount received was $15,905,557.76.

The net revenue from customs during the year ending on the 1st of December, 1846, being the last year under the operation of the tariff act of 1842, was $22,971,403.10, and the net revenue from customs during the year ending on the 1st of December, 1847, being the first year under the operations of the tariff act of 1846, was about $31,500,000, being an increase of revenue for the first year under the tariff of 1846 of more than $8,500,000 over that of the last year under the tariff of 1842.

The expenditures during the fiscal year ending on the 30th of June last were $59,451,177.65, of which $3,522,082.37 was on account payment of principal and interest of the public debt, including Treasury notes redeemed and not funded. The expenditures exclusive of payment of public debt were $55,929,095.28.

It is estimated that the receipts into the Treasury for the fiscal year ending on the 30th of June, 1848, including the balance in the Treasury on the 1st of July last, will amount to $42,886,545.80, of which $31,000,000, it is estimated, will be derived from customs, $3,500,000 from the sale of the public lands, $400,000 from incidental sources, eluding sales made by the Solicitor of the Treasury, and $6,285,294.55 from loans already authorized by law, which, together with the balance in the Treasury on the 1st of July last, make the sum estimated.

The expenditures for the same period, if peace with Mexico shall not be concluded and the Army shall be increased as is proposed, will amount, including the necessary payments on account of principal and interest of the public debt and Treasury notes, to $58,615,660.07. On the 1st of the present month the amount of the public debt actually incurred, including Treasury notes, was $45,659,659.40. The public debt due on the 4th of March, 1845, including Treasury notes, was $17,788,799.62, and consequently the addition made to the public debt since that time is $27,870,859.78.

Of the loan of twenty-three millions authorized by the act of the 28th of January, 1847, the sum of five millions was paid out to the public creditors or exchanged at par for specie; the remaining eighteen millions was offered for specie to the highest bidder not below par, by an advertisement issued by the Secretary of the Treasury and published from the 9th of February until the 10th of April, 1847, when it was awarded to the several highest bidders at premiums varying from one-eighth of per cent to 2 per cent above par. The premium has been paid into the Treasury and the sums awarded deposited in specie in the Treasury as fast as it was required by the wants of the Government.

To meet the expenditures for the remainder of the present and for the next fiscal year, ending on the 30th of June, 1849, a further loan in aid of the ordinary revenues of the Government will be necessary. Retaining a sufficient surplus in the Treasury, the loan required for the remainder of the present fiscal year will be about $18,500,000. If the duty on tea and coffee be imposed and the graduation of the price of the public lands shall be made at an early period of your session, as recommended, the loan for the present fiscal year may be reduced to $17,000,000. The loan may be further reduced by whatever amount of expenditures can be saved by military contributions collected in Mexico. The most vigorous measures for the augmentation of these contributions have been directed and a very considerable sum is expected from that source. Its amount can not, however, be calculated with any certainty. It is recommended that the loan to be made be authorized upon the same terms and for the same time as that which was authorized under the provisions of the act of the 28th of January, 1847.

Should the war with Mexico be continued until the 30th of June, 1849, it is estimated that a further loan of $20,500,000 will be required for the fiscal year ending on that day, in case no duty be imposed on tea and coffee, and the public lands be not reduced and graduated in price, and no military contributions shall be collected in Mexico. If the duty on tea and coffee be imposed and the lands be reduced and graduated in price as proposed, the loan may be reduced to $17,000,000, and will be subject to be still further reduced by the amount of the military contributions which may be collected in Mexico. It is not proposed, however, at present to ask Congress for authority to negotiate this loan for the next fiscal year, as it is hoped that the loan asked for the remainder of the present fiscal year, aided by military contributions which may be collected in Mexico, may be sufficient. If, contrary to my expectation, there should be a necessity for it, the fact will be communicated to Congress in time for their action during the present session. In no event will a sum exceeding $6,000,000 of this amount be needed before the meeting of the session of Congress in December, 1848.

The act of the 30th of July, 1846, "reducing the duties on imports," has been in force since the 1st of December last, and I am gratified to state that all the beneficial effects which were anticipated from its operation have been fully realized. The public revenue derived from customs during the year ending on the 1st of December, 1847, exceeds by more than $8,000,000 the amount received in the preceding year under the operation of the act of 1842, which was superseded and repealed by it. Its effects are visible in the great and almost unexampled prosperity which prevails in every branch of business.

While the repeal of the prohibitory and restrictive duties of the act of 1842 and the substitution in their place of reasonable revenue rates levied on articles imported according to their actual value has increased the revenue and augmented our foreign trade, all the great interests of the country have been advanced and promoted.

The great and important interests of agriculture, which had been not only too much neglected, but actually taxed under the protective policy for the benefit of other interests, have been relieved of the burdens which that policy imposed on them; and our farmers and planters, under a more just and liberal commercial policy, are finding new and profitable markets abroad for their augmented products. Our commerce is rapidly increasing, and is extending more widely the circle of international exchanges. Great as has been the increase of our imports during the past year, our exports of domestic products sold in foreign markets have been still greater.

Our navigating interest is eminently prosperous. The number of vessels built in the United States has been greater than during any preceding period of equal length. Large profits have been derived by those who have constructed as well as by those who have navigated them. Should the ratio of increase in the number of our merchant vessels be progressive, and be as great for the future as during the past year, the time is not distant when our tonnage and commercial marine will be larger than that of any other nation in the world.

Whilst the interests of agriculture, of commerce, and of navigation have been enlarged and invigorated, it is highly gratifying to observe that our manufactures are also in a prosperous condition. None of the ruinous effects upon this interest which were apprehended by some as the result of the operation of the revenue system established by the act of 1846 have been experienced. On the contrary, the number of manufactories and the amount of capital invested in them is steadily and rapidly increasing, affording gratifying proofs that American enterprise and skill employed in this branch of domestic industry, with no other advantages than those fairly and incidentally accruing from a just System of revenue duties, are abundantly able to meet successfully all competition from abroad and still derive fair and remunerating profits. While capital invested in manufactures is yielding adequate and fair profits under the new system, the wages of labor, whether employed in manufactures, agriculture, commerce, or navigation, have been augmented. The toiling millions whose daily labor furnishes the supply of food and raiment and all the necessaries and comforts of life are receiving higher wages and more steady and permanent employment than in any other country or at any previous period of our own history.

So successful have been all branches of our industry that a foreign war, which generally diminishes the resources of a nation, has in no essential degree retarded our onward progress or checked our general prosperity.

With such gratifying evidences of prosperity and of the successful operation of the revenue act of 1846, every consideration of public policy recommends that it shall remain unchanged. It is hoped that the system of impost duties which it established may be regarded as the permanent policy of the country, and that the great interests affected by it may not again be subject to be injuriously disturbed, as they have heretofore been by frequent and sometimes sudden changes.

For the purpose of increasing the revenue, and without changing or modifying the rates imposed by the act of 1846 on the dutiable articles embraced by its provisions, I again recommend to your favorable consideration the expediency of levying a revenue duty on tea and coffee. The policy which exempted these articles from duty during peace, and when the revenue to be derived from them was not needed, ceases to exist when the country is engaged in war and requires the use of all of its available resources. It is a tax which would be so generally diffused among the people that it would be felt oppressively by none and be complained of by none. It is believed that there are not in the list of imported articles any which are more properly the subject of war duties than tea and coffee.

It is estimated that $3,000,000 would be derived annually by a moderate duty imposed on these articles.

Should Congress avail itself of this additional source of revenue, not only would the amount of the public loan rendered necessary by the war with Mexico be diminished to that extent, but the public credit and the public confidence in the ability and determination of the Government to meet all its engagements promptly would be more firmly established, and the reduced amount of the loan which it may be necessary to negotiate could probably be obtained at cheaper rates.

Congress is therefore called upon to determine whether it is wiser to impose the war duties recommended or by omitting to do so increase the public debt annually $3,000,000 so long as loans shall be required to prosecute the war, and afterwards provide in some other form to pay the semiannual interest upon it, and ultimately to extinguish the principal. If in addition to these duties Congress should graduate and reduce the price of such of the public lands as experience has proved will not command the price placed upon them by the Government, an additional annual income to the Treasury of between half a million and a million of dollars, it is estimated, would be derived from this source. Should both measures receive the sanction of Congress, the annual amount of public debt necessary to be contracted during the continuance of the war would be reduced near $4,000,000. The duties recommended to be levied on tea and coffee it is proposed shall be limited in their duration to the end of the war, and until the public debt rendered necessary to be contracted by it shall be discharged. The amount of the public debt to be contracted should be limited to the lowest practicable sum, and should be extinguished as early after the conclusion of the war as the means of the Treasury will permit.

With this view, it is recommended that as soon as the war shall be over all the surplus in the Treasury not needed for other indispensable objects shall constitute a sinking fund and be applied to the purchase of the funded debt, and that authority be conferred by laws for that purpose. The act of the 6th of August, 1846, "to establish a warehousing system," has been in operation more than a year, and has proved to be an important auxiliary to the tariff act of 1846 in augmenting the revenue and extending the commerce of the country. Whilst it has tended to enlarge commerce, it has been beneficial to our manufactures by diminishing forced sales at auction of foreign goods at low prices to raise the duties to be advanced on them, and by checking fluctuations in the market. The system, although sanctioned by the experience of other countries, was entirely new in the United States, and is susceptible of improvement in some of its provisions. The Secretary of the Treasury, upon whom was devolved large discretionary powers in carrying this measure into effect, has collected and is now collating the practical results of the system in other countries where it has long been established, and will report at an early period of your session such further regulations suggested by the investigation as may render it still more effective and beneficial.

By the act to "provide for the better organization of the Treasury and for the collection, safe-keeping, and disbursement of the public revenue" all banks were discontinued as fiscal agents of the Government, and the paper currency issued by them was no longer permitted to be received in payment of public dues. The constitutional treasury created by this act went into operation on the 1st of January last. Under the system established by it the public moneys have been collected, safely kept, and disbursed by the direct agency of officers of the Government in gold and silver, and transfers of large amounts have been made from points of collection to points of disbursement without loss to the Treasury or injury or inconvenience to the trade of the country.

While the fiscal operations of the Government have been conducted with regularity and ease under this system, it has had a salutary effect in checking and preventing an undue inflation of the paper currency issued by the banks which exist under State charters. Requiring, as it does, all dues to the Government to be paid in gold and silver, its effect is to restrain excessive issues of bank paper by the banks disproportioned to the specie in their vaults, for the reason that they are at all times liable to be called on by the holders of their notes for their redemption in order to obtain specie for the payment of duties and other public dues. The banks, therefore, must keep their business within prudent limits, and be always in a condition to meet such calls, or run the hazard of being compelled to suspend specie payments and be thereby discredited. The amount of specie imported into the United States during the last fiscal year was $24,121,289, of which there was retained in the country $22,276,170. Had the former financial system prevailed and the public moneys been placed on deposit in the banks, nearly the whole of this amount would have gone into their vaults, not to be thrown into circulation by them, but to be withheld from the hands of the people as a currency and made the basis of new and enormous issues of bank paper. A large proportion of the specie imported has been paid into the Treasury for public dues, and after having been to a great extent recoined at the Mint has been paid out to the public creditors and gone into circulation as a currency among the people. The amount of gold and silver coin now in circulation in the country is larger than at any former period.

The financial system established by the constitutional treasury has been thus far eminently successful in its operations, and I recommend an adherence to all its essential provisions, and especially to that vital provision which wholly separates the Government from all connection with banks and excludes bank paper from all revenue receipts.

In some of its details, not involving its general principles, the system is defective and will require modification. These defects and such amendments as are deemed important were set forth in the last annual report of the Secretary of the Treasury. These amendments are again recommended to the early and favorable consideration of Congress.

During the past year the coinage at the Mint and its branches has exceeded $20,000,000. This has consisted chiefly in converting the coins of foreign countries into American coin.

The largest amount of foreign coin imported has been received at New York, and if a branch mint were established at that city all the foreign coin received at that port could at once be converted into our own coin without the expense, risk, and delay of transporting it to the Mint for that purpose, and the amount recoined would be much larger.

Experience has proved that foreign coin, and especially foreign gold coin, will not circulate extensively as a currency among the people. The important measure of extending our specie circulation, both of gold and silver, and of diffusing it among the people can only be effected by converting such foreign coin into American coin. I repeat the recommendation contained in my last annual message for the establishment of a branch of the Mint of the United States at the city of New York.

All the public lands which had been surveyed and were ready for market have been proclaimed for sale during the past year. The quantity offered and to be offered for sale under proclamations issued since the 1st of January last amounts to 9,138,531 acres. The prosperity of the Western States and Territories in which these lands lie will be advanced by their speedy sale. By withholding them from market their growth and increase of population would be retarded, while thousands of our enterprising and meritorious frontier population would be deprived of the opportunity of securing freeholds for themselves and their families. But in addition to the general considerations which rendered the early sale of these lands proper, it was a leading object at this time to derive as large a sum as possible from this source, and thus diminish by that amount the public loan rendered necessary by the existence of a foreign war.

It is estimated that not less than 10,000,000 acres of the public lands will be surveyed and be in a condition to be proclaimed for sale during the year 1848.

In my last annual message I presented the reasons which in my judgment rendered it proper to graduate and reduce the price of such of the public lands as have remained unsold for long periods after they had been offered for sale at public auction.

Many millions of acres of public lands lying within the limits of several of the Western States have been offered in the market and been subject to sale at private entry for more than twenty years and large quantities for more than thirty years at the lowest price prescribed by the existing laws, and it has been found that they will not command that price. They must remain unsold and uncultivated for an indefinite period unless the price demanded for them by the Government shall be reduced. No satisfactory reason is perceived why they should be longer held at rates above their real value. At the present period an additional reason exists for adopting the measure recommended. When the country is engaged in a foreign war, and we must necessarily resort to loans, it would seem to be the dictate of wisdom that we should avail ourselves of all our resources and thus limit the amount of the public indebtedness to the lowest possible sum.

I recommend that the existing laws on the subject of preemption rights be amended and modified so as to operate prospectively and to embrace all who may settle upon the public lands and make improvements upon them, before they are surveyed as well as afterwards, in all cases where such settlements may be made after the Indian title shall have been extinguished.

If the right of preemption be thus extended, it will embrace a large and meritorious class of our citizens. It will increase the number of small freeholders upon our borders, who will be enabled thereby to educate their children and otherwise improve their condition, while they will be found at all times, as they have ever proved themselves to be in the hour of danger to their country, among our hardiest and best volunteer soldiers, ever ready to attend to their services in cases of emergencies and among the last to leave the field as long as an enemy remains to be encountered. Such a policy will also impress these patriotic pioneer emigrants with deeper feelings of gratitude for the parental care of their Government, when they find their dearest interests secured to them by the permanent laws of the land and that they are no longer in danger of losing their homes and hard-earned improvements by being brought into competition with a more wealthy class of purchasers at the land sales. The attention of Congress was invited at their last and the preceding session to the importance of establishing a Territorial government over our possessions in Oregon, and it is to be regretted that there was no legislation on the subject. Our citizens who inhabit that distant region of country are still left without the protection of our laws, or any regularly organized government. Before the question of limits and boundaries of the Territory of Oregon was definitely settled, from the necessity of their condition the inhabitants had established a temporary government of their own. Besides the want of legal authority for continuing such a government, it is wholly inadequate to protect them in their rights of person and property, or to secure to them the enjoyment of the privileges of other citizens, to which they are entitled under the Constitution of the United States. They should have the right of suffrage, be represented in a Territorial legislature and by a Delegate in Congress, and possess all the rights and privileges which citizens of other portions of the territories of the United States have heretofore enjoyed or may now enjoy.

Our judicial system, revenue laws, laws regulating trade and intercourse with the Indian tribes, and the protection of our laws generally should be extended over them.

In addition to the inhabitants in that Territory who had previously emigrated to it, large numbers of our citizens have followed them during the present year, and it is not doubted that during the next and subsequent years their numbers will be greatly increased.

Congress at its last session established post routes leading to Oregon, and between different points within that Territory, and authorized the establishment of post-offices at "Astoria and such other places on the coasts of the Pacific within the territory of the United States as the public interests may require." Post-offices have accordingly been established, deputy postmasters appointed, and provision made for the transportation of the mails.

The preservation of peace with the Indian tribes residing west of the Rocky Mountains will render it proper that authority should be given by law for the appointment of an adequate number of Indian agents to reside among them.

I recommend that a surveyor-general's office be established in that Territory, and that the public lands be surveyed and brought into market at an early period.

I recommend also that grants, upon liberal terms, of limited quantities of the public lands be made to all citizens of the United States who have emigrated, or may hereafter within a prescribed period emigrate, to Oregon and settle upon them. These hardy and adventurous citizens, who have encountered the dangers and privations of a long and toilsome journey, and have at length found an abiding place for themselves and their families upon the utmost verge of our western limits, should be secured in the homes which they have improved by their labor. I refer you to the accompanying report of the Secretary of War for a detailed account of the operations of the various branches of the public service connected with the Department under his charge. The duties devolving on this Department have been unusually onerous and responsible during the past year, and have been discharged with ability and success.

Pacific relations continue to exist with the various Indian tribes, and most of them manifest a strong friendship for the United States. Some depredations were committed during the past year upon our trains transporting supplies for the Army, on the road between the western border of Missouri and Santa Fe. These depredations, which are supposed to have been committed by bands from the region of New Mexico, have been arrested by the presence of a military force ordered out for that purpose.

Some outrages have been perpetrated by a portion of the northwestern bands upon the weaker and comparatively defenseless neighboring tribes. Prompt measures were taken to prevent such occurrences in future.

Between 1,000 and 2,000 Indians, belonging to several tribes, have been removed during the year from the east of the Mississippi to the country allotted to them west of that river as their permanent home, and arrangements have been made for others to follow.

Since the treaty of 1846 with the Cherokees the feuds among them appear to have subsided, and they have become more united and contented than they have been for many years past. The commissioners appointed in pursuance of the act of June 27, 1846, to settle claims arising under the treaty of 1835-36 with that tribe have executed their duties, and after a patient investigation and a full and fair examination of all the cases brought before them closed their labors in the month of July last. This is the fourth board of commissioners which has been organized under this treaty. Ample opportunity has been afforded to all those interested to bring forward their claims. No doubt is entertained that impartial justice has been done by the late board, and that all valid claims embraced by the treaty have been considered and allowed. This result and the final settlement to be made with this tribe under the treaty of 1846, which will be completed and laid before you during your session, will adjust all questions of controversy between them and the United States and produce a state of relations with them simple, well defined, and satisfactory. Under the discretionary authority conferred by the act of the 3d of March last the annuities due to the various tribes have been paid during the present year to the heads of families instead of to their chiefs or such persons as they might designate, as required by the law previously existing. This mode of payment has given general satisfaction to the great body of the Indians. Justice has been done to them, and they are grateful to the Government for it. A few chiefs and interested persons may object to this mode of payment, but it is believed to be the only mode of preventing fraud and imposition from being practiced upon the great body of common Indians, constituting a majority of all the tribes. It is gratifying to perceive that a number of the tribes have recently manifested an increased interest in the establishment of schools among them, and are making rapid advances in agriculture, some of them producing a sufficient quantity of food for their support and in some cases a surplus to dispose of to their neighbors. The comforts by which those who have received even a very limited education and have engaged in agriculture are surrounded tend gradually to draw off their less civilized brethren from the precarious means of subsistence by the chase to habits of labor and civilization.

The accompanying report of the Secretary of the Navy presents a satisfactory and gratifying account of the condition and operations of the naval service during the past year. Our commerce has been pursued with increased activity and with safety and success in every quarter of the globe under the protection of our flag, which the Navy has caused to be respected in the most distant seas.

In the Gulf of Mexico and in the Pacific the officers and men of our squadrons have displayed distinguished gallantry and performed valuable services. In the early stages of the war with Mexico her ports on both coasts were blockaded, and more recently many of them have been captured and held by the Navy. When acting in cooperation with the land forces, the naval officers and men have performed gallant and distinguished services on land as well as on water, and deserve the high commendation of the country.

While other maritime powers are adding to their navies large numbers of war steamers, it was a wise policy on our part to make similar additions to our Navy. The four war steamers authorized by the act of the 3d of March, 1847, are in course of construction.

In addition to the four war steamers authorized by this act, the Secretary of the Navy has, in pursuance of its provisions, entered into contracts for the construction of five steamers to be employed in the transportation of the United States mail "from New York to New Orleans, touching at Charleston, Savannah, and Havana, and from Havana to Chagres;" for three steamers to be employed in like manner from Panama to Oregon, "so as to connect with the mail from Havana to Chagres across the Isthmus;" and for five steamers to be employed in like manner from New York to Liverpool. These steamers will be the property of the contractors, but are to be built "under the superintendence and direction of a naval constructor in the employ of the Navy Department, and to be so constructed as to render them convertible at the least possible expense into war steamers of the first class." A prescribed number of naval officers, as well as a post-office agent, are to be on board of them, and authority is reserved to the Navy Department at all times to "exercise control over said steamships" and "to have the right to take them for the exclusive use and service of the United States upon making proper compensation to the contractors therefor."

Whilst these steamships will be employed in transporting the mails of the United States coastwise and to foreign countries upon an annual compensation to be paid to the owners, they will be always ready, upon an emergency requiring it, to be converted into war steamers; and the right reserved to take them for public use will add greatly to the efficiency and strength of this description of our naval force. To the steamers thus authorized under contracts made by the Secretary of the Navy should be added five other steamers authorized under contracts made in pursuance of laws by the Postmaster-General, making an addition, in the whole, of eighteen war steamers subject to be taken for public use. As further contracts for the transportation of the mail to foreign countries may be authorized by Congress, this number may be enlarged indefinitely.

The enlightened policy by which a rapid communication with the various distant parts of the globe is established, by means of American built sea steamers, would find an ample reward in the increase of our commerce and in making our country and its resources more favorably known abroad; but the national advantage is still greater-of having our naval officers made familiar with steam navigation and of having the privilege of taking the ships already equipped for immediate service at a moment's notice, and will be cheaply purchased by the compensation to be paid for the transportation of the mail in them over and above the postages received.

A just national pride, no less than our commercial interests, would Seem to favor the policy of augmenting the number of this description of vessels. They can be built in our country cheaper and in greater numbers than in any other in the world.

I refer you to the accompanying report of the Postmaster-General for a detailed and satisfactory account of the condition and operations of that Department during the past year. It is gratifying to find that within so short a period after the reduction in the rates of postage, and notwithstanding the great increase of mail service, the revenue received for the year will be sufficient to defray all the expenses, and that no further aid will be required from the Treasury for that purpose.

The first of the American mail steamers authorized by the act of the 3d of March, 1845, was completed and entered upon the service on the 1st of June last, and is now on her third voyage to Bremen and other intermediate ports. The other vessels authorized under the provisions of that act are in course of construction, and will be put upon the line as soon as completed. Contracts have also been made for the transportation of the mail in a steamer from Charleston to Havana.

A reciprocal and satisfactory postal arrangement has been made by the Postmaster-General with the authorities of Bremen, and no difficulty is apprehended in making similar arrangements with all other powers with which we may have communications by mail steamers, except with Great Britain.

On the arrival of the first of the American steamers bound to Bremen at Southampton, in the month of June last, the British post-office directed the collection of discriminating postages on all letters and other mailable matter which she took out to Great Britain or which went into the British post-office on their way to France and other parts of Europe. The effect of the order of the British, post-office is to subject all letters and other matter transported by American steamers to double postage, one postage having been previously paid on them to the United States, while letters transported in British steamers are subject to pay but a single postage. This measure was adopted with the avowed object of protecting the British line of mail steamers now running between Boston and Liverpool, and if permitted to Continue must speedily put an end to the transportation of all letters and other matter by American steamers and give to British steamers a monopoly of the business. A just and fair reciprocity is all that we desire, and on this we must insist. By our laws no such discrimination is made against British steamers bringing letters into our ports, but all letters arriving in the United States are subject to the same rate of postage, whether brought in British or American vessels. I refer you to the report of the Postmaster-General for a full statement of the facts of the case and of the steps taken by him to correct this inequality. He has exerted all the power conferred upon him by the existing laws.

The minister of the United States at London has brought the subject to the attention of the British Government, and is now engaged in negotiations for the purpose of adjusting reciprocal postal arrangements which shall be equally just to both countries. Should he fail in concluding such arrangements, and should Great Britain insist on enforcing the unequal and unjust measure she has adopted, it will become necessary to confer additional powers on the Postmaster-General in order to enable him to meet the emergency and to put our own steamers on an equal footing with British steamers engaged in transporting the mails between the two countries, and I recommend that such powers be conferred. In view of the existing state of our country, I trust it may not be inappropriate, in closing this communication, to call to mind the words of wisdom and admonition of the first and most illustrious of my predecessors in his Farewell Address to his countrymen.

That greatest and best of men, who served his country so long and loved it so much, foresaw with "serious concern" the danger to our Union of "characterizing parties by geographical discriminations-Northern and Southern, Atlantic and Western-whence designing men may endeavor to excite a belief that there is a real difference of local interests and views," and warned his countrymen against it.

So deep and solemn was his conviction of the importance of the Union and of preserving harmony between its different parts, that he declared to his countrymen in that address:

It is of infinite moment that you should properly estimate the immense value of your national union to your collective and individual happiness; that you should cherish a cordial, habitual, and immovable attachment to it; accustoming yourselves to think and speak of it as of the palladium of your political safety and prosperity; watching for its preservation with jealous anxiety; discountenancing whatever may suggest even a suspicion that it can in any event be abandoned, and indignantly frowning upon the first dawning of every attempt to alienate any portion of our country from the rest or to enfeeble the sacred ties which now link together the various parts.

After the lapse of half a century these admonitions of Washington fall upon us with all the force of truth. It is difficult to estimate the "immense value" of our glorious Union of confederated States, to which we are so much indebted for our growth in population and wealth and for all that constitutes us a great and a happy nation. How unimportant are all our differences of opinion upon minor questions of public policy compared with its preservation, and how scrupulously should we avoid all agitating topics which may tend to distract and divide us into contending parties, separated by geographical lines, whereby it may be weakened or endangered.

Invoking the blessing of the Almighty Ruler of the Universe upon your deliberations, it will be my highest duty, no less than my sincere pleasure, to cooperate with you in all measures which may tend to promote the honor and enduring welfare of our common country.

www.ingramcontent.com/pod-product-compliance
Lightning Source LLC
Chambersburg PA
CBHW070844290526
45795CB00002B/978